IMAGES OF ENGLAND

AROUND
STAPLETON

IMAGES OF ENGLAND

AROUND
STAPLETON

VERONICA SMITH

TEMPUS

I should like to dedicate this book to the memory of two dear friends, Steve Brown and Mike Purnell. Steve was killed in a road accident on 1 May 2002. He was thirty-six years old. He was a kind, amusing and dependable man and the massive attendance at his funeral demonstrated his immense popularity.

Mike was the driving force behind the Easton reunions and will be sadly missed by his many friends. He has helped me on innumerable occasions with information for my books for which I shall always be grateful. His widow, my friend Claudine, has kindly loaned me photographs relating to his important contribution to the Royate Hill campaign, the story of which is told within the pages of this book.

Frontispiece: The marriage of Gloria Pearce and Melvyn Hoare, Stapleton church, 1960.

First published 2003

Tempus Publishing Limited
The Mill, Brimscombe Port,
Stroud, Gloucestershire, GL5 2QG
www.tempus-publishing.com

British Library Cataloguing in Publication Data.
A catalogue record for this book is available from the British Library.

ISBN 0 7524 3059 9

Typesetting and origination by Tempus Publishing Limited.
Printed in Great Britain by Midway Colour Print, Wiltshire.

Contents

Stapleton church from Bell Hill, 1920.

Introduction

I must explain at the outset that this is not a definitive history of Stapleton village and its surrounds. It is a pictorial history of people who lived there in the twentieth century on lands once owned by prominent families – the Beauforts, the Smythes and the Harfords. Their names and backgrounds are perpetuated in the roads that were built on their land. Cotterell Road and Dormer Road, for instance, are surnames of members of the Smythe clan, and Rousham, Tackley and Heyford were Oxfordshire villages where they had their roots.

The area covered within this book was all at one time part of the estate of the Dukes of Beaufort, and all the development charted here has taken place in little over a hundred years. It seems, as time goes by, that everything is visibly speeding up. We live in a throwaway society and sometimes even our buildings seem transitory. An example of this is Maytrees Home for the Blind at Eastville, built on the site of the old workhouse. It seems it had hardly become part of the local landscape when it was razed to the ground.

I have particularly enjoyed writing this book because I moved to Ingmire Road when I was seven and grew up there. Because my friends from next door, the Hopton family, moved to Stapleton, that too became familiar territory and I attended Sunday school and enrolled with the Girl Guides at the chapel on Broom Hill. I remember working for my Tracking badge on the rocky paths by Snuff Mills quarry under the supervision of Captain (Miss Lisle) and 'Leftie' who was also a Sunday school teacher. I was in the Nightingale Patrol.

I do hope you will all find something in these pages to stir some memories, maybe a name, a face from the past or a scene which has vanished forever. Please forgive any omissions. I am only able to work from the photographs which people have been kind enough to put at my disposal. If you feel there are important stories left to tell and have relevant pictures please get in touch as the area is a fascinating one to me and could well warrant a further book at some later date.

Acknowledgements

Firstly I must particularly thank Margaret and Dave Harris and Melvyn and Gloria Hoare for providing the original photographs in this collection and giving me the impetus to forge ahead and seek out the rest of the material which makes up this book. A debt of gratitude, too, to Syd and Audrey Marks for stepping in at the eleventh hour and providing some absolute gems which made the publication complete. I would also like to acknowledge the kindness and help of the headmistress and staff of Glenfrome Road School, Pam Fursman, Mrs T. Havill, Ray Bulmer, Donald and Sheila Belsten, Dorothy Lloyd, Vi Andrews, Ruby Maggs, Jenny Thomson, John Street, Jane Bradley, Local History Studies at Bristol Central Library, Hilary at Muller Road Library, Keith Evans, David Stone, Margaret Smailes, Alison and staff at Bristol Records Office, Doreen Redmore, Mollie Finch, Peter Hobday, Pat Gerrish and to Gerry Brooke at the *Evening Post*. Thanks, also, to Grace Cooper for sourcing extra photographs.

Special thanks also to Mike Hooper who worked so hard on my behalf making photographic copies for me.

one

Origins

Stapleton's antiquity is demonstrated by the fact it is actually recorded in the Domesday Book. At that time it was in the manor of Barton. In 1086 the village was recorded as possessing 2,554 acres, in contrast to Bristol itself which, in this period, was composed of a mere 1,717. In 1174 William, Earl of Gloucester gave part of the manor, including his lands at Stapleton and the fishing rights of the River Frome, to Tewkesbury Abbey. It was in this period that a church is first mentioned as existing there. The font in the west porch is all that remains of that church, which was dedicated to St Giles.

In the late sixteenth century reference is made to a vicarage, and a school must have come into being around that era as a Richard Cable is recorded as being the schoolmaster.

A replacement church was built in 1691 and dedicated to the Holy Trinity. The patronage of the parish in this period belonged to Thomas Walter of Heath House. It later passed to the Smythe family through marriage.

The present church was consecrated on 15 April 1857. It took three years to construct and the architect was John Norton. It provides an impressive sight from all aspects.

Stapleton church from the Park Road direction.

Stapleton House. This elegant property was lost in the 1930s and the land used to build modern housing.

The skyline is dominated by Stoke House in its beautiful setting, the grassy slopes seen here with cattle grazing. This was destined, together with Heath House and Beech House (formerly Stapleton Grove), to form the basis for Stoke Park Colony. The system was based on one operating in Germany devised to care and provide training for children with learning difficulties. Revd Harold Burden pioneered this scheme in Bristol. He had originally come to the city to take up an appointment as Chaplain at Horfield prison.

A view of Heath House, now hidden behind the M32. This once belonged to the Smythe family, and Sir John chose to live here rather than at Ashton Court. The road which leads to the house is still known as Sir John's Lane. It later came into the possession of the Cotterell Dormer family.

Left: Everyone made a beeline for Duchess Park at Easter – it was a perfect place to picnic and to roll your painted hard-boiled eggs down the hill.

Below: A dramatic view of Stoke House, with a ghostly figure patrolling one of the terraces!

Above: The gates to the estate. The Ranger's house used to be situated near this entrance. It was known as Stoke Lodge. It was a most attractive building, especially at night when the light glowed through the lead-paned windows. It was regrettably demolished in the 1960s.

Below: A spectacular view of Duchess Pond – although the term 'pond' is something of an understatement. Inexplicably those in authority decided to fill it in during the 1960s, but recently the decision was reversed and all was restored to its former glory.

In the early nineteenth century Stapleton was a Mecca for artists. Francis Danby painted this view of the River Frome, *c.* 1823.

The appearance of the church is rather unprepossessing in this 1854 sketch by Revd Symons.

Right: A photograph of the church taken from the cottages at the top of Wickham Hill.

HOLY TRINITY, STAPLETON, BRISTOL.

Below: The church was a wonderful setting for a wedding. Some girls, including the author's mother, Violet Ellery, seen here at her wedding to Harold Peck of Bournemouth in 1936, even lodged in the parish while the banns were called to ensure the perfect setting for a fairytale occasion.

This is the wedding of Sheila Screen and Donald Belsten in April 1955. The bridesmaids are, from left to right: Esme Belsten, sister of the groom; Janet and Margaret Hoare, the bride's cousins; Margaret Belsten, another sister of the groom; Patsy Keegan, cousin of the bride and Eileen Brookman.

From bridesmaid to bride. This time, on 28 March 1959, it is Margaret Hoare who is the bride, marrying David Harris from Welsford Avenue. The best man is Garth Dyer and the bridesmaids are Linda, David's twin (on the left), and Janet, Margaret's sister.

WICKHAM BRIDGE, WICKHAM GLEN, STAPLETON, BRISTOL.

There has always been an ambience about Wickham Glen, a strange brooding atmosphere, heightened perhaps by the mist which hangs suspended a few feet above the ground some twilit evenings. Sometimes you'd swear you hear the tramp of marching feet across the bridge as Cromwell and his men approach Wickham Court.

The little shops at the top of Bell Hill have served many purposes over the years but Popham's the newsagents was in existence longer than most. Their newspaper deliveries extended as far as Hambrook! This picture was taken in 1964.

Can a more dramatic and haunted scene be imagined than this view of Wickham Bridge, photographed by E. W. Twining in 1894?

Yet, on summer evenings, it could be the perfect romantic setting. Sheila Belsten, whose wedding we saw earlier in this chapter, perches on a stone wall in the glen, but will probably not be walking too far in those ankle strap shoes.

A sunlit corner of historic Wickham Court.

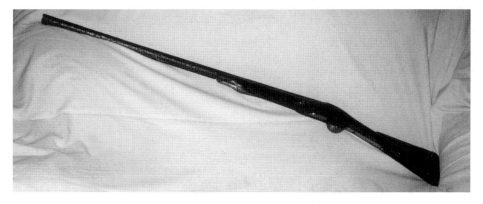

This is a gun dating from the time of the Civil War. Did Cromwell himself handle this weapon?

The road level has altered over the years but this row of cottages, pictured here in the 1920s, mercifully still exists at the bottom of Blackberry Hill.

'Frome Valley Stapleton Bristol' is the description on this postcard, with its vista of rolling hills and clusters of trees. Perhaps those of us who have spent our lives so close to these scenes need to step back sometimes to appreciate the sheer beauty of the place.

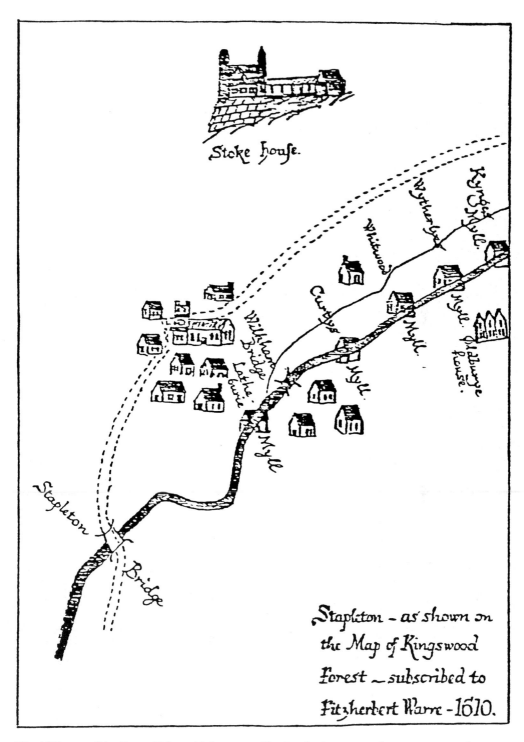

Stoke house.

Stapleton - as shown on the Map of Kingswood Forest ~ subscribed to Fitzherbert Warre - 1610.

The 1610 map of the Frome Valley with its many mills. Our forebears seemed to possess so much common sense, taking advantage of natural resources instead of striving to enforce their requirements on nature. Why is the same sort of logic not employed today?

45997.   OLDBURY COURT GARDENS.

This is the Oldbury Court end of the valley where a park was laid out in what had been the grounds of Oldbury Court, the mansion that was home to the Vassalls family.

This photograph of the mill at the Oldbury Court end of the valley was taken by E. W. Twining in 1894. The mill was already falling into disrepair.

Two more views of the mill as it slowly disintegrates, the first taken by W. Cole in 1901, the second from a card postmarked June 1906. There are still traces of the site visible today.

OLD SNUFF MILLS, STAPLETON.

E.T.W.D.

The history of the growth of the snuff industry is the subject of an extremely well-written article in the Alexandra Park School magazine. It was written by Margaret Belsten, a third-year pupil at Alexandra Park School in 1952. She tells us: 'Bristol was one of the great snuff-producing centres of the country and was surrounded by mills. In fact the manufacture of snuff proved such a paying business that millers who normally ground corn decided to grind snuff instead and in 1756 it was publicly announced by Bristol corporation that this conversion of the grist mills was becoming very detrimental to the public – they weren't getting enough flour to make their bread.' She speculates that perhaps one of these millers was the original 'Snuffy Jack', which is an interesting point.

The only remaining mill in the 'Snuff Mills' area, although ironically snuff was never ground here! It was purchased by the council and the part that was saved from total dereliction has become a tourist attraction.

Stepping Stones, Stapleton Glen,   Bristol.   218.

The entire area is a postcard vendor's dream. Dorcas sent this view to her friend in Cricklade in 1913 as she had visited the day before with 'Father and Aunt Pat'. 'Don't you think it pretty?' she asks.

This is a really pretty scene – when the river froze over in 1964.

It has always been an excellent place for courting too, as young Mel Hoare and Gloria Pearce discovered back in the 1950s. Here they are seen standing near the quarry, with Mel's impressive motorbike behind them.

DUCHESS POND AND WALK, STAPLETON, BRISTOL.

A tranquil scene looking down towards Stoke House.

A view from long ago with the weir looking rather dangerous…

…and in its sunnier moments.

This is a dramatic scene. There is a look of unrest about the river.

The river can be unpredictable here, as when it burst its banks in 1966. On the corner of Frome Place clearance has begun for the road-widening scheme. The shop has already disappeared.

Floods are a big adventure for young Donna Hoare.

And even the adults can't resist splashing about.

All the residents are out in force to witness the drama.

A smartly suited Mel Hoare surveys the scene in the days when River View boasted two shops – Short's off-licence and Hill's the grocers. Both these stores have since been converted for domestic use.

This is the same view as the previous photograph but taken on a summer's day. It is sad that the shops closed down.

Outcome of a romance in River View. Pictured in front of Mr James' house in Broom Hill are Frank Golledge and Nan Shepherd, who lived next to the chapel in River View. Among the guests can be seen Mr James himself, who ran the dairy, also his wife Joyce and daughter Susan. Also celebrating the occasion are neighbours Mr and Mrs Herbert Hoare and Mr and Mrs Frank Hoare. Walt Green can be seen in the doorway.

February 1963 and snow still lingers where Blackberry Hill meets Broom Hill. The shop on the corner of Frome Place – once referred to as Green's, then Ashford's, and latterly Hill's – is still trading but was later lost to a road-widening scheme and one more piece of history disappeared.

These picturesque cottages were also a casualty of the demand for more road space. It is these stealthy alterations which slowly but surely erode the fabric of the landscape.

Looking down Broom Hill in 1961. Many changes have taken place since then. New houses and flats have sprung up by Duchess's Gate and the Trendlewood estate has been established. Yet, in spite of everything, Stapleton retains its unique character.

A view across the valley: Stapleton in its rural splendour in the 1960s. Even Wickham Court has a mellow appearance in the sunlight of this moment.

A Loxton sketch of 'Bristol Police Orphanage, Stapleton, about 1910.' But where was this institution?

A Fred Orchard advertisement in the form of a blotter to inform present and potential customers of his services. Actually, paraffin stoves were extremely efficient and cost-effective.

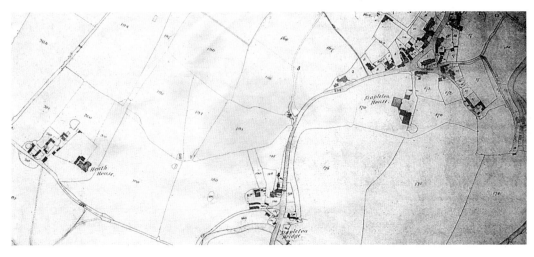

A tithe map of the area dating from the mid-nineteenth century. Studying the ownership and leasing records of the fields and properties is fascinating, not least for the number of old Stapleton names which emerge – Absalom Bisp (house and windmill), Robert Hopton (house and garden), Samuel, Charles and John Breddy (landowners) – making one aware of the continuity of life in the village. The whole area is steeped in history – surely there must be some ghosts? Does Cromwell still pace the paths of Wickham Glen debating his next strategy? Does Mary Lewis, slain for financial gain by her actor son-in-law Charles Barrett in 1836 in Lypiatts Lane (now Brinkworthy Road), still shed tears for her grieving daughter Sarah? There is a presence here which makes itself felt.

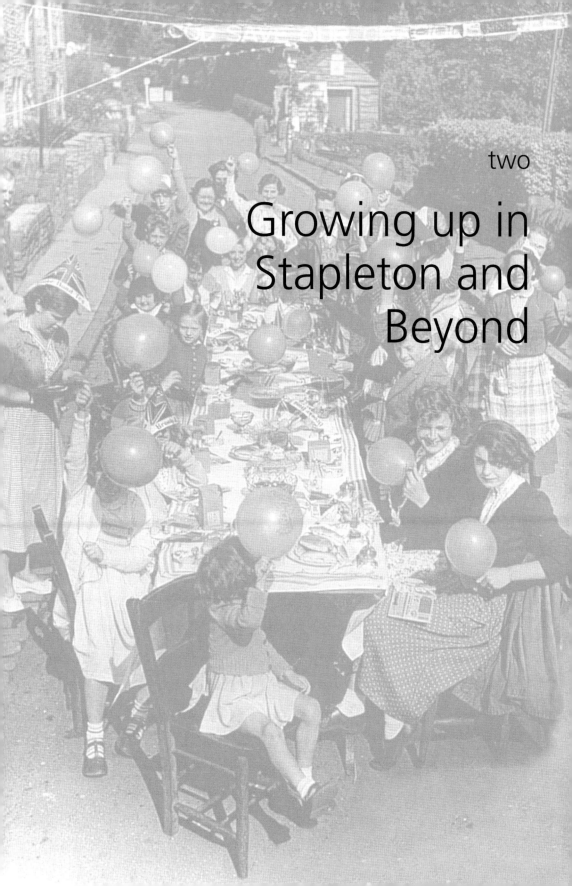

two

Growing up in
Stapleton and
Beyond

It is sad that today's children will never know the freedom that earlier generations enjoyed. Nowadays there are so many hazards to cope with – the ever-increasing volume of traffic, drug culture and its associated financing through crime and prostitution and a far more fragmented society. Families no longer stay within the confines of a village or a district, which minimises the chances of a strong support network in times of trouble. Divorce rates increase annually and many children must often wonder where their loyalties lie. There is pressure on them to mature ever more rapidly, meaning that the innocence of childhood so many of us remember covers a far shorter span than ever before.

In this chapter we look back to times when, although money may not have been plentiful, children had a sense of identity and security. They may have had to run constant errands, wear hand-me-downs and rarely, if ever, go on holiday, but the structure and fabric of their lives gave them a feeling of continuity and belonging.

Local sporting heroes line up with the man in charge, Frank Hoare. From left to right, back row: Frank Hoare, Dave Harvie, Mike Goodwin, Mike Levitt, Keith Brown, -?-, Don McArthur, Eric Gay. Front row: -?-, Mel Hoare, P. Evans, Colin Hibbert, John Faithfull.

Top: Another sporting line-up under the tutelage of Bob Prescott, standing on the right, and Frank Hoare, assistant manager, on the left. From left to right, back row: Gordon Bisp, J.Shears, -?-, P. Gazzard, Don McArthyur, A. Pinker. Front row: -?-, ? Hooper, Eric Gay, Alan Jones, Colin Branton, Mel Hoare, -?-.

Middle: Stapleton Colts pictured in the 1954/55 season. This under-16 team won their league that year. The senior AFC team also had an impressive record. They were champions of Division One of the local amateur league in 1959/60, 1960/61, 1961/62 and runners-up in 1962/63. In the Premier Combination, Division Two they were champions 1963/64. The line-up is, from left to right, back row: Frank Hoare (assistant manager), Dave Trubody, Colin Branton, Alan Frost, K. Francombe, D. Harvie, -?-, Barry Flook, Bob Prescott (manager). Front row: P. Evans, S. Turner, Don McArthur, -?-, Mel Hoare.

Bottom: Vassalls Park football team, with management, on their home pitch in the early 1950s. From left to right, back row: George Andrews, Pete Moulding, Jack Paterson, Frank Hoare, George Allen, Phil Johns, ? Harrold, ? Bradley, -?-, Douglas McDowell, Sam Bird, -?-, Bob Prescott, -?-, ? Pearce, Dave Lear, Brian Curtis, Bert Hiscocks, Ron Waites. Second row: Alan Walters, Tony Moulding, -?-, Wilf Worgan, -?-, Jeff Danks, Charlie Miller, ? Goodenough, ? Taylor (president), Bert Belsten (chairman), -?-, Reg Mundy, John Alexander, 'Brummy'. Front row: ? Evans, Gordon Bisp, ? Hooper, -?-, Eric Gay, ? Jones, ? Gazzard, ? Branton, ? MacArthur, Mel Hoare, A. Pinker, ? Solomon.

Some familiar names in this line-up, From left to right, back row: C. Clements, C. Branton, M. Case, G. Clarke, A. Frost, D. Davis, -?-. Front row: T. Upton, C. Hibbert, D. Harvie, J. Faithfull.

Here we have Begbrook Youth Club gathered together in the late 1950s. Among the familiar faces are G. Hazell, Clive Iles, Martin Graydon, Roger Sansom, Mel Hoare, Rich Gomerson, Mel Rogers, Dave Fox, Rich Poole, Denis Greaves, Mike Kimber, John Hillard, Mel Maggs, Alan Naish, Mike Hawthorne, Pete Higgins, Brian Curtis, Barry Crew, Pete Temblett, Alan Ford, Mrs Abbot, Mr Abbot, Mrs Jefferies, Alf Ford, Mr Paul and Mr Crew.

Savers' Club Christmas party, 1952. The people pictured include Mrs Porter, Mrs Habb, Mrs Price, Mrs Gubb, Mrs E. Wheeler, Mrs Milliner, Mrs W. Maggs holding Brian, Mr and Mrs Shone, Mrs Cambridge, Mrs Mattens with Paul, Mrs Waites with Alan, members of the Belsten family, Mel Hoare. Others, pictured sitting and standing in the centre of the picture, are G. Nash, J. Shone, D. Preddy, A. Dove, ? Stinchcombe, two of the Cambridge family, Kay Hammerfield, D. Wheeler, S. Ham, H. Milliner, M. Maggs, M. Evans, M. Perkins, S. Harrington, J. Price, G. Pearce, M. Gubb and B. Turton.

Coronation day party in River View. The lady in the check pinny with the balloons is Nelly Green. The dark-haired girl in the spotted skirt is Margaret Belsten, author of the piece on Snuff Mills quoted in the last chapter. Next to her is Glynis Green. Further up the table on the right we have Brian Cook and his sister, and at the top of the table, in the smart leather jacket, Mel Hoare. The group at the back include Mrs Ashford, Mrs Kinchin and Mrs Delph Hall. On the left-hand side of the table can be seen Mr Billy Hall, Mrs Cook, Glenys Pickett, Alan Waites and Michael Hawthorne.

Alexandra Park's football team on their home pitch with All Saints church in the background. The only name known in this group is Roger Tomlin, third from left on the back row. The picture was taken in 1963. In later years Roger joined Bristol Constabulary where he won a medal for bravery.

Claverham Road, Fishponds, puts on a fancy-dress parade for Coronation day, 1953. Some hard work has clearly gone into making these costumes.

More scenes from the same party. Some of the children look a bit bewildered.

Over at Glebe Gardens, Frenchay, another party is in progress.

Tables have been pushed together and everyone has brought out chairs, tablecloths and cutlery.

More fancy dress and fun and games on the grass between the prefabs, which were erected as a temporary measure to ease the housing shortage after the Second World War but lasted much longer than anticipated. They disappeared in the early 1960s but in other parts of Bristol some are still in use today.

Another Christmas Savings Club party at Stapleton in 1952. Among those pictured are
Mr R. Hoare and Anita, Mrs Maggs, Mrs Guppy, treasurer Mr Hobby, Mr Frank Hoare, Bert
Belsten, Charlie Miller, Mr and Mrs Moulding, Mrs Maud Evans, Mrs Betty Hoare, Esme
Belsten, Mrs Dyer, ? Wisten, Jeffrey Hunter, Brian Curtis, Mel Hoare, Trevor Hoare, Mike
Goodwin, Maggie Belsten, Hilda Milliner, Maureen Evans, June Price, two members of the
Erwin family, Alan Dove, George Nash, Melvyn Maggs, Heather Price, Jill Price, Cherry Tanner,
Maurice Gubb, Suzanne McDonald, Diane May and Bob Mann.

This faded photograph has been included because of its rarity value. It shows a class at Chester Park
School in 1929 with teachers Miss Francombe and Miss Penquinney (on the left).

Begbrook Junior School – a picture from the 1950s. The only names known are: R. Thomas, B. State, N. Williams, S. Pearce, S. Belsher, D. Leggett, Pamela Priddle, S. Tanner, M. Stevens.

Alexandra Park School, which was the main secondary school for the children of Stapleton. The school finally closed in July 1987.

A class from the 1930s showing John Street (third from left, front row) and classmates. Although it is not particularly clear it is included as there are few remaining photographs of the school from this era.

In the 1940s now, and Class 3a pictured on 9 April 1947. From left to right, back row: D. Winstone, K. Evans, E. Longford, D. Breddy, E. Walker, A. Williams, R. Leonard. Second row: D. Evans, V. Hall, J. Perry, B. Peacock, P. Dutton, C. Bracey, D. Woodhouse. In the front row sits 'Bulldog' Turner flanked by V. Shears and P. Bees on the left and J. Hobbs and M. Porter on the right.

This lovely picture of the Oldbury Court School nativity play taken in 1956 or 1957 shows Jenny Tomlin as the angel with the shining halo. The little girl clutching *Our Bedtime Story Book* was called Naomi. Jenny recalls that a number of the children attending the school at that time were from the Downend Homes, a type of Barnardo's institution.

Here is Jenny again, far left by the radiator, in crisp white blouse and cardigan, when she was at Fishponds Infants School the following year. It must be Christmas to judge by the nativity scene on the wall and cut-out Christmas trees beneath the window. A paper chain suspended on the far wall is evidence of another fun project.

A step back in time now to other children having fun. These little ones were performing the ribbon dance at Fishponds Carnival in 1913.

These lads are hard at work basket-making in the arts and crafts class at Dr Bell's, Fishponds. This picture dates from 1929 or 1930.

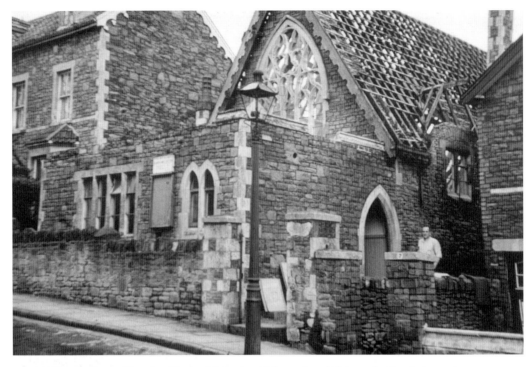

Above: Stapleton Church of England School, which stood on Brinkworthy Road. As can be seen here, the process of demolition has already begun.

Below: Local historian Syd Marks took this photograph of the school hall just prior to its final destruction. The school closed in the 1960s.

Right: Glynis Green (left) and a friend, with the school in the background. They are standing on the corner of Lynn Road.

Below: The school hall with pupils standing on the stage at the back. This was the retirement party for Mr Barrett, the headmaster. The picture dates from the 1950s.

Above: A picture of Standards One and Two taken in the 1920s. None of the pupils' names are known, so if any of them are reading this book, identification would be greatly welcomed.

Left: Pauline Curtis, top right, and other members of the Stapleton Guide Troop sample life under canvas, late 1940s. Janet Vowles is also pictured.

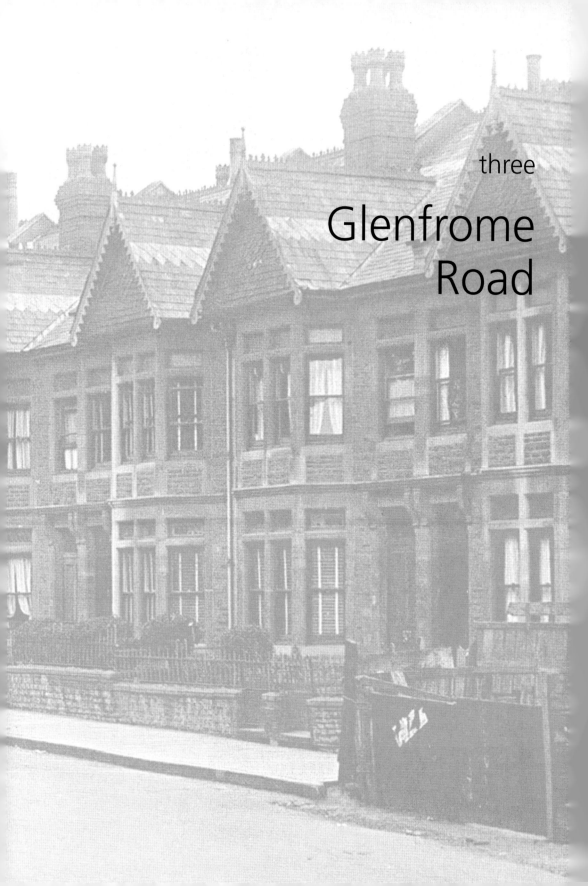

three

Glenfrome Road

G lenfrome Road was developed in the early 1930s. Formerly it had been Wee Lane, a byway which had meandered from St Werburgh's all the way to Bridge Farm, which stood, as it still does, at the bottom of Bell Hill. The Withers family live there now as they did then.

The Merchants Arms was established in the late 1930s to serve the influx of new residents. Houses were going up where the fields had once stretched down from the Bishop's Palace to the riverbanks. Welsford Road and Avenue and Averay Road came into being with neat little roads intersecting. They had pretty landscaped gardens and a small row of shops.

VE Day celebrations as the residents of Welsford Avenue and Road lay on a splendid spread. Among the throng are Mrs Florence Harris and her twin children David and Linda. Her husband, Bill, was in the RAF.

Above: Before the motorway came the Bell Hill/Glenfrome Road junction provided an attractive view, but now the scene is marred by ugly concrete pillars. The houses on the left, up Bell Hill, just glimpsed behind the trees, have now gone in favour of a modern development and a road which leads to more new houses.

Left: A peaceful scene from 1952 showing Stapleton church from the high ground in the park. Averay Road can be seen in the middle distance. It was named after Sir John Averay, a Merchant Venturer who once owned the land.

The floods of 1968. A pick-up truck ploughs through the water at the bottom of Bell Hill.

The elegant houses facing Eastville Park when the row was known as Park Terrace. It all looks very tranquil and leisurely.

A warm August day in 1957, perhaps a Sunday as there seem to be fathers taking the children out for an afternoon on the lake.

The boathouse, with a queue forming for the paddle boats – a favourite treat for the younger children.

Timothy Marks is in the centre of this picture, taken in 1978. He certainly seems to be enjoying the experience.

The approach to Cotterell Road through the park, a view lost forever since the advent of the M32. How could the residents of these properties ever have envisaged a time when the relentless rumbling rhythm from the roadway overhead would haunt their days and nights?

If we followed the 139 bus route (it later became the 19) along that winding way that was once Wee Lane we would pass under the railway bridge that carried the goods trains. The bus that travelled this route was of necessity a single-decker as the bridge was so low. This is the view looking towards St Werburgh's as demolition begins.

This is looking from the opposite side of the bridge. It can clearly be seen in this shot just how little headroom there was.

The building of the new school in Glenfrome Road caused a stir of excitement as most of the children in the area had never seen such a spectacle. We were all used to crumbling stone edifices with lavatories in the playground and high narrow windows through which all we could see was sky. We watched with great interest as progress was made. In this picture we have Mr Bioletti's class from 1955. It seems to have been a rather windy day. From left to right, back row: -?-, -?-, Stephen ?, Robert Withers, Geoff Cox, Martin Hart, -?-, -?-, -?-. In the next row, from left to right, are -?-, Geoff Dilley, Stephen Brown, Janet Owen, -?-, -?-, Helen Skinner, Geraldine Ball, Sheila Martin, -?-, ? Thomas, Phil Caines. Seated in the next row are Linda Sanders, -?-, -?-, Linda ?, -?-, Kath Williams, -?-, -?-, Marlene Haywood, Diane Hughes. In the front are -?-, Barry Charles, -?-, -?-, Morley Martin.

A sunny day in 1957 and Mr Raymond Verrier's class pose on the slopes of Purdown. From left to right, back row: Christopher Monks, Billy ?, Derek Williams, Steve Allen, Trevor Denley, Barry Charles, -?-, Paul Woods, Philip Hodges, Mervyn Skuse, Roger Wood. In front of this group are Brent Sage, Graham Plumley, -?-, -?-, -?-, Suzanne Hole, Gillian Curtis, Jeannette Philpotts, Katherine ?, -?-, Janet Owen, David Long, David Harvey and Alan Pratley. Of the girls seated in the front the only names known are Maureen Blower (third from the left) and Jean-May Curtis (extreme right).

Still in 1957 and this class stand by the picture windows of the school in front of which a border of hollyhocks can be seen. From left to right, back row: -?-, -?-, Trevor Denley, Peter Hunt, Barry Charles, Clive Courtney (?), Paul Wood (?), Alan Fullick, Philip Hodges. Second row: -?-, -?-, -?-, -?-, Suzanne Hole, -?-, Jeannette Philpotts, Pamela Osborne, Barbara Pearce, -?-, Dorcas Penry. Third row: -?-, Heather Pinnegar, -?-, -?-, Maureen Blower, -?-, -?-, Susan Cross, -?-. Front row: Les Whitmore, Alan Pratley, Peter ?, -?-, -?-, Timothy Shippobotham (?), Roger Wood, Frank Dacey.

Mr Ford's class in 1958 all look very happy to be having a break from lessons. From left to right, back row: Paul Bailey, Philip Hodges, -?-, Steve Addey, Paul Wood (?), Barry Charles, Trevor Denley, Peter Hunt, Stephen Allan. Second row: Danny Ware, Derek Williams, Dorcas Penry, Cath Foxwell, Jeannette Perry, Gillian Curtis, Suzanne Hole, Kathleen Isaac, Janet Owen, Roger Wood, Brent Sage. Third row: Barbara Pearce, Heather Pinnegar, Susan Cross, Pamela Osborne, -?-, -?-, Maureen Blower, -?-, -?-. Front row: Michael Evans, Alan Pratley, David Harvey, David Long, Mervyn Skuse, Chris Monks.

This is Miss Griffee's class in June 1959. From left to right, back row: Martin Duckham, -?-, -?-, Paul Gardner, -?-, John ?, Maurice Copin, -?-, Alan Mees, -?-, -?-, Thomas Havill. Next row, seated, are Jacqueline Long, Elizabeth Dring, Anne Charles, Helen Thomas, Pat ?, Andrea Bowaman, Georgina Capel, Jacqueline ?, Patricia McElroy. In front of them sit Christine Tremlett, -?-, Diane Price, Sheila Balch, Judith Harvey, Anne Foxwell, Susan Boyce, Nadine Cartwright. Front row: -?-, Robert ?, John Hyde, -?-, Christopher Hale, Guy Shippobotham, Melvyn Barnes.

It is 1959 and the children congregate in the playground for their class photographs. From left to right, back row: Timothy Shippobotham, -?-, Paul Wood, Alan Fullick, Clive Courtney, Patrick Fursman, Paul Dickinson, Keith Willey, Frank Dacey. The only names known of the children in the second row are the two on the extreme right – Mary Dring and Jean-May Curtis. Third row: Denise Lumsden, -?-, -?-, -?-, -?-, June Bartlett, Marilyn Dibbin, -?-, Marie Grant. Front row: Les Whitmore, Barry Able, Donald McCloud, Graham Plumley, Richard Salter, -?-.

Only one child in this group has been identified in this group from 1962 and that is Nicholas Lanceley, on the extreme left, second row.

Mr Bennett's class of 1963. It must have rained that day as the pupils have assembled in the hall for their photograph. From left to right, back row: Stephen Shepherd, Stephen Brown, John Whitmore, Christopher Brown, Neil ?, Graham Pavey, Stephen ?, Dennis Davey, Martin Thomas, Philip Jones, -?-. Second row: Sandra Clark, Rosemary York, Christine Fullick, Esther Hards, Margaret ?, ? Howell, Jillian Sweeney, Linda Hawkins, Christine Thomas, Janice Burt. Third row: Hilary Clouter, Alison Heard, ? Ducklin, Alison Smith, Jane Edwards, Jane Gollop, Lesley Bradford, Valerie Cox, Frances Palmer, Patricia ?. Front row: John Sanders, Michael Fisher, Philip Britton, David Reynolds, Bryan Balson, Mark Lamborn, Paul Tomlinson, -?-, -?-.

1963 and another class positions itself outside the school. From left to right, back row: Keith ?, Royston Newell, Martin Sandford, Nicholas Lanceley, Peter ?, Billy Peverly, Laurence Bath, Pete Willis. Second row: -?-, -?-, Gayle Holland, ? Hicks, -?-, Lois Davies, Linda Golledge, Angela ?, -?-, -?-, Claire ?, Richard Fuller, Gerald Hawkins. Third row: -?-, Michael Notton, Andrew Edwards, -?-, -?-, Rebecca Flay, -?-, -?-, Front row: Robin Butterworth, Andrew Caple, Michael Merrick, -?-, -?-, -?-, Chris Williams, -?-, -?-, -?-.

Only a few pupils from this class of 1964 can be identified. From left to right, back row: -?-, -?-, Mike Merrick, Phil Walters, -?-, Nicholas Lanceley, -?-, Peter Wills. Chris Williams is pictured in the second row.

four

Muller Road

M uller Road came into being in the 1920s, when it was called simply New Road. Then, for a brief while, it was known as Dormer Road. In 1926 the only houses there were two small rows on opposite sides of the road, near the Stapleton Road crossroads. There were also twenty-five properties in Cotterell Road built in a similar style.

The 1930s saw a sudden upswing in society. Houses began to spring up, smart semis and terraces comprising small sections of houses separated by lanes running along the backs of the gardens. Space was the keyword and Muller Road and its offshoots fulfilled all the criteria demanded – pleasant views, proximity to Eastville Park and Purdown, three bedrooms, two receptions, kitchen, bathroom and gardens front and rear. Those who could afford to left behind the constriction of narrow Easton streets for a life in the leafy suburbs.

New Road, Eastville.

This is all there was of Muller Road prior to the building boom of the 1930s.

Where there are houses you will find potential customers. A little row of shops went up on the first slope before reaching Glenfrome Road. Here we see Havill's bakery with young Reginald Havill and his sister who worked for their father. Later Reginald ran the shop with his wife Audrey. Next door can be glimpsed Cannicott's, the paper shop. The shop is still run as a newsagents today. The other shops trading at the outset were a grocer's, a drapery store, a greengrocer and two ladies' hairdressers.

This is a unique snapshot from, it is believed, the 1920s. The players in fancy dress are, from left to right: H. Bailey, I. Scott, R. Pursey and (possibly) M. Bailey. These tennis courts were on the lower slopes of Purdown. In the background can be seen the Thirteen Arches, St Thomas' church and houses in Stapleton Road and Cotterell Road. Eastville Park Methodist church can just be seen behind the houses. The tennis party were members of the church and always used these courts. The exact location of the courts can be seen in the photograph below. It is believed that the picture was taken by Miss Clarice Fursman, a stalwart member of the church.

This is the view from the back bedroom of 235 Glenfrome Road. These houses were built in 1932 and the gardens are beginning to look established so this is probably 1933 or 1934. To the right of the picture the lines of the tennis court can be seen, and nestling in the trees is a little cottage known as the Lodge, where an old couple lived without water, sanitation or electricity. It is thought it was previously used by employees of the Heath House estate. Heath House itself can be glimpsed through the trees to the left on the horizon. On the middle ground, Heyford Avenue was built later in the 1930s.

Members of the church enjoying an outing. It looks as though they are gathered near the tennis court. Among those enjoying the afternoon is young Cyril Fursman, the little boy in the light suit and Eton collar, second row from the back, near the tree. In later years he played the organ for the Primitive Wesleyan chapel at Eastville and was well known as a piano tuner, looking after those at the Colston Hall. His father stands behind and a little to the right wearing a stock and with his back to the tree. His mother is also in the back row but towards the other end, wearing a huge dark picture hat. Clarice Fursman, Cyril's sister, stands in the group to the left, next to a young mother with a boater holding her baby. The photograph was taken around 1913 or 1914.

All mod cons. Susan and Christine Hopton share a bath in their Ingmire Road home. The old-fashioned geysers could prove tricky to light! This property was one of the ones built by their father, R. J. (Jack) Hopton.

A wide lane with garages and space for children to play safely on their tricycles and scooters. This is the author's mother pictured in the lane behind Ingmire Road in 1959. Nowadays there are security gates at each land entrance, unimaginable in the free and easy fifties.

In this particular lane there was the added attraction of a railway embankment and an inviting wall to climb next to the entrance to Wide Gates, the house supplied by the Bristol Gas Company to its local manager. In the 1950s the manager was Mr Ross and the beautiful house where his family lived had lovely grounds and a tennis court. The archway can still be seen near the Tesco roundabout but the house to which it once led is long gone. It was approximately where Burger King stands today.

Washing blowing on the line, so time for a chat over the garden wall. The author's mother exchanges gossip with Dorrie Pane from No. 11.

Birthday parties were simple affairs in those pre-bouncy castle days – just sandwiches and jellies and lemonade, then off to play in the garden or lane. Here are the Hopton girls, Susan and Christine, front left; and Margaret and Catherine, back right; with children who include Beryl Johnson, Shirley May and Audrey Arrowsmith, whose parents ran the Maypole dairy on Stapleton Road.

Further up the hill the Lockleaze estate was being developed in the late 1940s on the far slopes of Purdown. Here the road layouts have been marked in preparation for construction.

Meanwhile other plans were afoot for the ground at the back of Tackley Road. Excitement stirred as the residents realised they were going to get a library, the first to be built for many a year. The progress of the building was followed with fascination by the entire neighbourhood.

Every day some subtle addition would be noted.

Finished at last!

The official opening took place on Friday 29 December 1950. The Lord Mayor performed the ceremony.

The library was an absolute boon for everyone in the area. Children from the local school were invited to come and see what was on offer.

The children look entranced.

Alas all bubbles are fated to burst and this explosion took the form of the news that a motorway was to be built which would alter the face of Muller Road. Initially the plans did not alarm too much. Minor changes, perhaps, but the elegant structure of the Thirteen Arches viaduct would be preserved and only a few properties would be lost... The reality was to be much, much harsher.

five

Major
Changes

The building of the M32 was probably one of the most cataclysmic changes to the area encompassed by the boundaries of Eastville. It is hard to know where the area begins and ends but for the purposes of this book it extends from Berwick Road to Averay Road and from Glenfrome Road to Royate Hill. Along the way it merges into Easton, Fishponds, Greenbank and St Werburgh's.

In retrospect the devastation seemed to begin with the demolition of the famous Thirteen Arches but that was not really the case. We had already lost a few shops and houses, and then, insidiously, small pockets of development began to mushroom over the next fifteen years. Buildings which we thought would be there forever began to slide away, unnoticed sometimes until they had actually gone. Would it be paranoid to suggest stealth methods were employed? Judge for yourselves when you have read the chapter on Royate Hill.

But to return to the Muller Road area where it really began:

The first signs of events to come. The corner of Muller Road is being cleared in preparation for the M32 roundabout.

The shops on the corner, a newsagents and a grocery store, have gone along with two houses, Nos 610 and 612. The garage on the opposite corner, next to the gabled house seen in the foreground, is also in the process of being removed. It had a wide-windowed café-cum-shop at the top of a sweeping flight of stone steps and sold Tizer, Lyons ice cream and Fruitie ice lollies to thirsty children returning from hot afternoons in the park.

The bridge has been blown up and the houses seen in the previous picture are gone, although the backs of the remaining houses on 'Lower' Stapleton Road enjoy a temporary stay of execution. In one of these tall houses lived, in the 1960s, a West Indian man who used to sit in his doorway playing a guitar and singing 'The Old Rugged Cross'.

A view showing the ground being levelled. Some interesting cars of the era can be seen speeding along Muller Road, among them a couple of Austin A40s and a Ford Anglia

The 'new' houses fared no better than their more mature neighbours. These dream homes of the 1930s, Nos 678, 680 and 682 Muller Road, fell to clear the path of progress in November 1976. The remainder would be spared a few years longer.

The Viaduct Garage had already served its last gallon of petrol some years earlier. The back of a Triumph Herald can be seen at the side. Next door is the house that had belonged to Griffee's the builders.

Above: The forecourt. In those days you could sit in your car and wait for an attendant to fill the tank. It was here in the late 1940s that the son of the owner died tragically in an accident involving a lorry.

Right: An aerial view showing the roundabout being laid out and the pillars being sunk to support the overhead structure. The location can be pinpointed by using the chapel at the junction of Stapleton Road and Fishponds Road as a guide.

The motorway is now well established and changes are taking place at Eastgate where Tesco is nearing completion. It was opened in May 1986 in torrential rain and the stockroom flooded!

A look back now to what was there before. These were the kennels at the stadium in the days when dogs were actually kept on-site. In later years they were kennelled at their trainers' bases and brought to the track on the day of the race. These buildings, with their corrugated iron roofs, were not ideal for housing dogs in hot weather. This picture was taken in November 1966. The Thirteen Arches, in the background, were demolished less than a year later.

Right: Some sort of presentation is taking place here at the stadium in December 1972.

Below: The last days of the stadium before it disappeared to make room for the Ikea store.

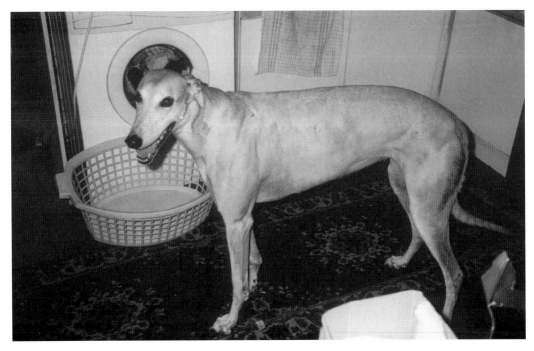

Ringside Wish, one of the last greyhounds to race at Eastville Stadium. Once an A1 dog, she rapidly adapted to domestic life.

Bristol Rovers' ground totally submerged in March 1947. Eastville was notorious for flooding but it was many years before a more efficient drainage system was installed to counteract the problems caused by the Frome bursting its banks.

More trouble at the stadium – this time fire was the problem. Here firemen struggle to contain the flames as the stand blazes. The year was 1980.

1983 and the Rovers are still drawing large crowds at Eastville. Many felt a lot of the charisma was lost when they relocated. The Rovers were synonymous with Eastville Stadium.

Eastville market in its heyday before it was forced to move to its present site. This photograph was taken in the summer of 1978.

There was always a tremendous atmosphere at the old market, with plenty of banter with the stallholders. Beyond the fence some demolition work seems to be taking place on the gasworks land. This picture was taken in 1971.

Another scene from 1971. Followers of fashion will be intrigued by the bouffant hairstyles and the collar detail on the jacquard coat worn by the customer puffing away on what was most likely an Embassy tipped.

This was the land owned by Bristol Gas Co. where the new offices are now, and where the market is now held. The picture probably dates from the early 1960s.

25 May 1979. The motorway is now a part of the landscape but the greyhound kennels are still in situ and the building of Tesco is still in the future.

With the volume of traffic increasing daily and the planned Eastgate centre nearing completion it was necessary to widen the bridge at the bottom of Muller Road.

Work was completed and the new bridge opened in December 1985.

Sometimes natural disasters happen to force changes. This is Sandy Lane, off Stapleton Road, in April 1984 when workmen had to demolish a collapsing house which was used as a storage area by CM Textiles, who had gone into liquidation.

The view down Glen Park to the little row of shops that disappeared when the motorway was built. There was a wide variety of goods on offer in these stores, which included a confectioner/newsagent, off-licence, ironmongers, fish and chip shop, a grocery business and a gentlemen's hairdresser. In the background looms the gasholder and the houses in Dormer Road.

At the top end of the street, on the Fishponds Road corner, stood the Beaufort Arms off-licence. It was later used as a wholesale clothing warehouse but at the time of writing is unoccupied, although renovations are taking place.

Glen Park in festive mood when war ended in 1945. Vi Andrews, one of the organisers, is seen in the centre of the picture with a bow in her hair, holding a milk jug.

Still in Glen Park, we see Vi Andrews again in the late 1940s. Her son Terry is proudly showing off his Cubs uniform.

A lovely picture of an old steam engine crossing the bridge by Fox Road. The year is 1962 and the River Frome still flows below, although somewhat contaminated by rubbish. The course of the river has since been diverted and the old river bed is now the foundation for a walkway.

Eastville Police Station boarded up and redundant in November 1973. Is it mere coincidence that crime has increased alarmingly since the decision to close such places was made?

September 1977. Eastville in the aftermath of an horrific explosion caused by a fire which began in the Raj restaurant. The six people who lived in the flats above were killed, including a teenage girl.

Eastville in 1982 after the removal of the Primitive Methodist chapel at the junction of Stapleton Road and Fishponds Road. A new office block has risen in its place. Among the shops, the post office is still trading and Bolloms is still in business. Bristol Knitwear's days were numbered – this was to be the site of the new job centre. The cake shop is already being demolished and the old fascia board is revealed showing it once was Frederick Warren's dining rooms.

Above: Eastville in the early years of the twentieth century. Shops included a tailor's, a baker's, a newsagents, a butcher's and an oyster bar. Now this section is rather run down, the only premises not given over to warehouses occupied by a launderette, a restaurant specialising in East African food and an advice bureau for Asian women.

Left: This is the Kelly's Directory entry for this section of road in 1926 from which can be seen that there was very little that could not be obtained in this few hundred yards!

328 STA BRISTOL AND SUBURBAN STREETS DIRECTORY.

Stapleton Road.
Lawford's Gate to Wee Lane.

[Parish—Holy Trinity, St. Philip's.
2 Hunt Thos. Edwd. city missionary
4 Dunn George
6 Brokenbrow William
8 Liddiard William Richmond
10 Watts Alfred
12 Constance William James, dentist
12 Constance Albert James, L.D.S.
 R.C.S.ENG. dental surgeon
 —Harleston Street intersects
14 Netcott Henry, watch maker
14 Netcott Henry, furniture dealer
16 Sweet Frank, bootmaker
18 Simmons Harold, hair dresser
20 Beehive Clothing Stores, cloth iers
 and gents' tailor
22 Beehive Clothing S ores, drapers
24 Portingale Charles Edward, glass
 & china shop
26 Nicholls John, greengrocer
28 Blackford Wm. Jn. furniture dlr.
30 Blackford Mrs Marie Louise,
 retail tobacconist
 —Winsford Street intersects
32 Pockett Leonard, Sea Horse, beer
 retailer
34 Holdon Walter, butcher
 CONGREGATIONALCHURCH&SCH LS.
36 Barnett Mrs A. E. milliner
38 Coombs Albert Frederick, ladies'
 and gents' tailor
40 Fox Miss Maud Jane, confectioner
42 British & Argentine Meat Co. ltd.
 butchers
44 Mills J. H. limited, grocers, etc.
46 Eastmans, limited, butchers
48 Lennards, limited, boot makers—
 George Henry Neale, manager
50 Lipton, limited, tea dealers
52 Hutton Edgar, hosier
54 Barns & Co. lim. ironmongers
 —Milsom Street intersects
56 Miel Barnett, draper
58 Salt William John, wholesale
 sundriesman
60 Ham Mrs Ellen, draper
62 Les Claude Melnotte, optician
64 Gray Geo. Wm. glass & china dlr.
66 & 68 Tonkin W. & Co. outfitters
70 { Warr George Herbert, stationer
 { Town Sun-Port & M.O. Office
72 Flower William, baker
74 Rankin Douglas, house furnisher
 —Webb Street intersects
76 Liddington Mrs Selina, baker
78 Webb G. H. provision curer
80 Coates Mrs Agnes, newsagent
82 Small Cyril W. butcher
84 to 90 Laues', drapers
92 Slade Herbert, news agent
94 Turner Mrs Al ce Leah, greengro.
 —Perry Street intersects
 [Parish—St. Gabriel.
96 Weeks Fdk. Geo. oil & color mer.
98 Witts George Albert, baker and
 confectioner
100 Brown Miss Elizh. tobacconist
102 Neale Arthur, grocer
104 Trump John, boot maker
106 Owen Miss Rose, butcher
108 Pincher John, greengrocer
110 W tkins Ernest Thomas,tobacnst.
112 Smith Ernest John, furniture dlr.
114 Luton E. & Son, bakers
 —Clark Street intersects
116 Strode Cook & Penfold, chemists
120 Adams Fred T. cycle agent
122 & 124 Goldstone William G. china
 and earthenware dealer
126 Wide Mrs Gertrude, draper
128 Buckle Harry, Post Office Tavern, b.r.
 —Armoury Square intersects
130 Adams Geo. Wm. Armoury Tav. v.
134 Reakes William, butcher
136 Singer Sewing Machine Co. ltd.
138 Fry Harold Lewis, dairyman
140 Watts Frank Hugh, stationer
142 Smith G. & Co. pork butchers
144 Tyrrell Charles William Harold,
 beer retailer
146 Knight Arthur John, hosier
 —Beaumont Street intersects
148 Watts Sidney G. confectioner
150 Williams James, watch & clock ma
152 Duffy Edmund, hardware dealer
154 Mills J. H. limited, grocers, etc.
156 Mason Mrs Winifred, milliner
158 Lewis Frederick Charles
158 Fisher Mrs Ann, draper
158a Clare Mrs Ethel Beatrice, milliner
160 Pigott Richard
160a Berry A. & Co. butchers
162 Bruce John
162a Pigott Richard, oyster bar
164 Benjamin Miss Rose
166 Ames Ernest, carriage proprietor
168 Orchard Chas. Wm. furn. remover.
170 Humphries Edward, garage
172 McCloskey Michael, L.R.C.P.Edin.,
 L.R.C.S., L.R.F.P.&Glas. surgeon
174 Tucker Henry Charles
176 Grant William, horse dealer
178 Oui-n Walt.r
180 Sage William Henry
 —Claremont Street intersects
182 Salter John Robert, general draper
184 Tovey Stanley, greengrocer
1 6 Bishop Tom, fried fish shop
190 Bristol Cycle Co.—Tom Thresh
 —Seymour Road intersects
 [Parish—St. Simon.
192 King Alfred Edward, chemist
192 Bowman Douglas, dentist
194 Johnson Brothers, lim ted, dyers
194 Goodwin Ernest, confectioner
196 Bennett Thos. picture frame mkr.
198 Tester Mss FlorenceAda,greengro.
200 Magrath Edwd.&Sons,pork btchrs.
202 Price Bros. (Bakers), ltd. bakers
202 Magrath Edward Joseph
204 Edmonds Stanley H. outfitter
206 Hatcher William, baker
 —KENSINGTON BAPTIST TABERNACLN.
208 Bristol Co—operative Society, ltd.
 grocers
210 Mead JosephBonfield, confectioner
212 Brooks Dye Works, limited
214 Henson Thomas William,stationer
214 Hart Harold, hairdresser
216 Barclays Bank, ltd.—R. W. Mus-
 grove, clerk in charge
218 Dibble Mrs Fanny Eliza, draper
220 Maypole Dairy Co., lim.
224 Greig David, provision dealer
224 Trubody Bros. wine and spirit dlr.
226 British & Argentine Meat Co.
 limited, butchers
228 Garlack Charles & Sons,ltd.hatters
 & hosiers
230 The Home & Colonial Stores, ltd.
232 Jefferis Evan, pork butcher
234 Charley's Drapery Co.
236 Star Supply Stores (The), grocers
 —George Gifford, manager
238 Miles Hy. James, general draper
240 Farrow & Co. ltd. butchers
242 Mills J.H.lim.grocers&prov. mers.
 —Kensington Park intersects
244 Eastmans, limited, butchers
246 Iles George Henry, fruiterer
248 Freeman, Hardy & Willis, limited,
 boot makers—C. J. G. Silk,mngr
250 Harding Miss Elizh. Jane, fruiterer
 —Oxford Place intersects
252 Fildes Fredk. J. hardware dealer
252a Sleigh Charles, watchmaker
252b, 254 & 256 Kelland & Co.furniture
 dealers
258 Walford Frank, baker
260 Sim kins Miss Mabel, dairy
262 Nott Walter George, Three Black-
 birds, vict.
 { HawsonMissKateR.postmistrss.
266 { Town Sun-Port, M. O. & T.
 { OFFICE
268 Burnell Mrs J. garage proprietor
268a Parson Norris H. umbrel'a maker
270 Lintern Fredk. Arthur, restaurant
274 Bennett Percy, fried fish dealer
276 Butt Mrs A. M. draper
278 Hollard Frederick, butcher
280 OppenheimMrsFlorence,tobacnst.
282 Seeley Miss Doris, milliner
284 Carter Ernest, tailor
286 & 288 Hodder Henry & Co. lim.
 chemists
286 Ham Edgar Merrick
 —Warwick Road & Warwick
 Avenue intersect
318 Milner Arthur M.B., B.Ch., B.A.O.
 physician and surgeon
318 Flood James Edward, M.B., B.Ch.,
 B.A.O. physician and surgeon
322 Gillard Mrs Mary
324 Stewart Alexander
326 Rawle Samuel Henry
328 Chimnick Willie Chapman
340 Baller George William Downing
332 Webber John Ford
334 Marshall Thomas
336 Lawrence Edward
338 & 340 Wyatt William James &
 Son, motor engineers
342 & 344 Crofts Francis, wood turner
346 F ench Harvey Lewis, tailor
348 Hulme George Percy, hair dresser
350 & 352 Swains Temperance Hotel
 —Fox Road intersects
352a White MrsElizh. wardrobe dealer
352b Wickham George Henry
354 Hobbs Mrs Mary, general shop
362 Price Bros. (Bakers), ltd. bakers
356 Major George Albert, baker
358 Bennett Stanley, confectioner
390 Pickett Charles
352 Witshell Mrs E. butcher
366 Ashman Ch rles J. furn. remover
370 Williams Albert Chas. newsagent
374 Howard James, boot repairer
374 Moon Herbert, dining rooms
376 Hall Mrs Bertha Elizh. grocery
378 Salter William Arthur, confectur.
380 Osborne Albt.Thos. Railway Inn,v.
382 Thompson Saml. & Sons, maltsters
 —Robert Street intersects
388 Andrews H. & Son, wire workers
 Wood King Co.ltd. firelighter mfrs.
388 Williams Joseph Henry, tailor
390 Cook Walter, baker
392 Oddy Joseph, news agent
394 Pople William Alfred, butcher
396 Morgan Henry Edgar, undertaker
398 Iles Isaac, hair dresser
400 Harris Mrs Selina, oyster bar
400 Boyce George, fruiterer
402 Godfrey Wm. F. tailors' trimmings
404 Garland Charles, harness maker
404 Garland Mrs Ellen, china & hardware dealer
406 Hodge Hugh, coffee tavern
408 Dodge Mrs Mary Ann, boot dealer
410 Woodward Walter John, butcher
412 Williams Joseph H. piano dealer
414 Pearks Dairies, Limited, stores
416 Allen Mark George, secondhand
 furniture dealer
418 Burnard A. & Co. tailors
422 Campbell Stanley C. tobacconist
424 Eastville Hippodrome Co. ltd.(the),
 cinematograph theatre

90

six

Up Fishponds Road

Superficially, perhaps, the changes along the road leading to Fishponds are less noticeable. It is only when you stop and consider how things once were that the losses are felt.

Probably the most significant alteration is the exchange of 100 Fishponds Road, once the dreaded workhouse, for a housing development with open-plan front gardens and all the roads named after herbs. There is also a health centre there, May Park School, and, until recently, a home for the blind.

It is probably easy to miss because the high stone wall remains, so it is only when you actually explore the territory that the changes are apparent. The old Coombe Road School vanished in the 1980s, and with it a fair few houses, to make way for the lighter, airier building that is May Park School.

There are now just a scattering of shops dotted along the road, whereas before there were clusters of trading premises serving local residents. Now that most families possess at least one car, a weekly trip to the supermarket has become the popular way to shop. Yet, in spite of this efficiency, folk seem to have far less time and are ten-times more stressed. So maybe a stroll along the road each day with a pencilled shopping list and a wickerwork basket was more conducive to a relaxed lifestyle than one would have thought.

3 October 1978 and John Wills, Lord Lieutenant of Avon and President of the Avon Talking Magazine Association for the Blind, opens the new soundproof studio at Maytrees residential home. Because of funding issues the home was forced to close in the 1990s, and it rapidly fell into disrepair. It was finally demolished in 2003.

This is 100 Fishponds Road after its transformation from workhouse to care home for the elderly. Here staff celebrate the end of the Second World War with a fancy-dress party. First prize went to Little Bo Peep in the front of the picture, next to Vi Andrews who came second in her oriental costume.

More celebrations at the home. This was taken in the same era. Here the staff are staging a show for the residents. Vi Andrews is fourth from the left, second row from the back. The matron is on the right-hand side of the front row dressed in knee breeches and accompanied by her pet dog.

These are the shops that faced the tall, bleak wall of the workhouse. The section in the centre of the photograph is that between Boswell Street and Glen Park. The Beaufort Arms off-licence was shown in more detail in the last chapter. The first six properties from the Boswell Street corner were demolished in the late 1960s to build a petrol station, and the next two were transformed into a car dealership. The rest of the block was given over to an auto parts dealer, an insurance broker's and an electrical contractors, so a large number of shops vanished almost overnight. Now the only domestic retailers in this part of Fishponds Road are a paper shop, an off-licence, a post office and a carpet shop. The sign on the lamp-post is interesting. It states: 'Electric trams stop here if required'.

We have candlelight, we have drinks – where are the girls? No, not a hopeful bunch in a singles bar, merely a power failure at the White Lion in December 1970.

Above: 102nd Bristol St Thomas Wolf Cubs pictured in 1940/41 assembling for parade.

Right: The Scouts join the youngsters as they prepare to march.

Everybody loves a parade. Here are the
St Thomas Scouts and Cubs leaving
St Mary's, Fishponds (*above*) and arriving at
Castle Green, Greenbank (*left*).

Below: The boys in Greenbank Road, all
very smartly turned out. The pictures date
from around 1970.

The 1959 wedding of Dorothy Tomlinson and David Lloyd at St Thomas' church. Some of the guests are reflected in the windows of the wedding car.

Same church, different era. This is the wedding of Iris and Wilf Marshall. Wilf's father was landlord of the Botany Tavern in Conduit Place, Lower Ashley Road. The little bridesmaid on the right married and moved to the United States where she raised six children.

An Easter bonnet parade seems to be in progress at St Thomas' church. The traditional Welsh headgear seems to be attracting some close scrutiny. The nervous-looking man with the balloon beret has to be the winner!

The Girls' Friendly Society at St Thomas' church enacting their 1953 production. In this on-stage shot Dorothy Tomlinson, in black lace shawl, conducts a lively exchange with a fellow thespian.

The entire cast poses for the camera.

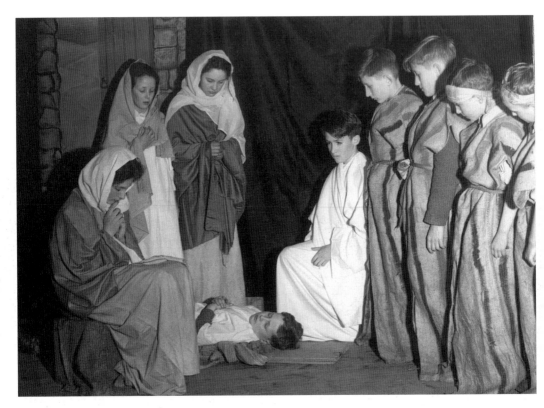

'Children in Gospel Production', ran the headline in the local paper. Seen here are some of the players in this mimed production of *They Led Him to be Crucified*. The cast included John Moore, whom the press described as portraying a 'serene Jesus'. Derek Blower was cast as Peter, Brian Robinson played Judas, Dorothy Tomlinson was Mary and Cicily Knight Martha. This 1950 production was considered remarkable inasmuch as the producer, the stage manager, reader and designers were all under eighteen.

A group of St Thomas parishioners pose with the choir shortly before the closure of the church. It was hoped that the beautiful wall panels might be removed and reused, but alas, it was not to be.

The wedding of Vi Nash and George Andrews in 1936. Here they are pictured outside the groom's parents' home in Coombe Road where the reception was held.

Eastville Park in 1905. There seems to be a predominance of important-looking men in hats. Was it a special occasion? The Queen's Head can be seen in the background.

A Loxton print of the park dating from 1911. The bandstand can be seen in the middle distance. It is sad this elegant structure was not preserved.

Eastville Park swimming pool in 1910. It is a great shame this was never restored.

Right: 14 Shamrock Road, one-time home to the Tomlinson family. This photograph taken by the original owner shows the house to be a fine example of 1930s architecture. It has the stained-glass top windows and brick-framed porch which give it the chic synonymous with this period of history.

Below: This is a unique photograph of Stonebridge Park on VE Day, with the visitors being entertained by a clown. Of fashion interest here are the wide-lapelled, belted coats, Cuban-heeled shoes and hats worn at jaunty angles.

Above: Marlborough House on the corner of Ridgeway Road and Marlborough Place. The name above the door is that of Frank William Osborne, who ran the shop from the 1930s until the 1960s. A beautiful street lamp from an earlier era stands on the pavement. The premises ceased to be used for commercial purposes in the 1980s and have since been converted for domestic use.

Left: This is the grandly-named Dunbar Castle in Berkeley Road. This was a long, narrow street which stretched from Fishponds Road through to Greenbank View. This area was flattened to make way for the grounds of May Park School.

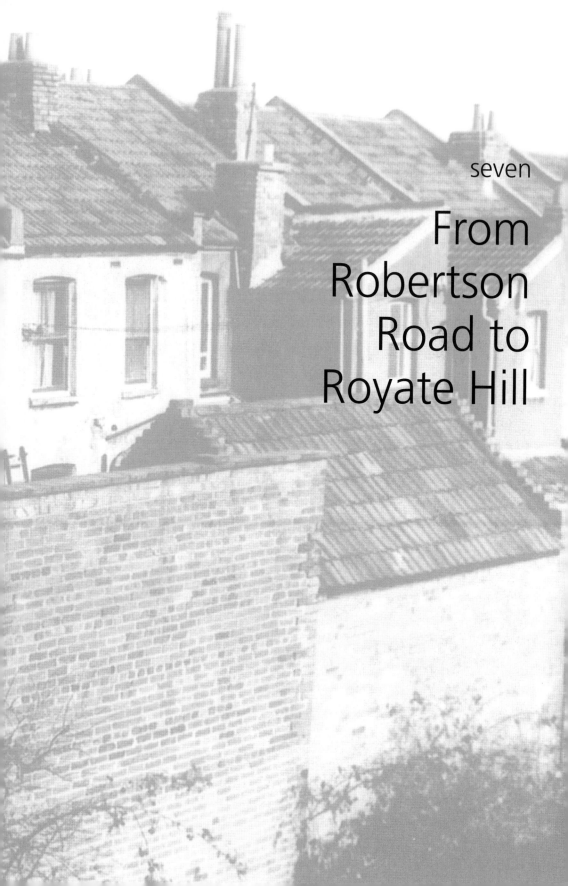

seven

From Robertson Road to Royate Hill

This area is perhaps the most unchanged we have visited, except that many of the corner shops have gone and now there are more shared houses and bedsits than family homes, but it does appear to have retained more of the ambience of times gone by. The area seems to attract people who are concerned about environmental issues. It was this stroke of providence that saved a threatened wildlife site. It happened thus: residents heard rumours that developers were planning to clear an embankment by the viaduct, which was a haven for wildlife. They formed an action group and campaigned relentlessly and thought they had succeeded when a public enquiry in December 1991 declared the site one of importance. However, using a legal loophole, the following May, on a bank holiday at dawn the contractors stealthily moved in and began to clear the site. The group converged there, pleading in vain for the drivers to stop. One woman even lay down in the path of a bulldozer. By the time a court injunction had been obtained to halt proceedings a third of the vegetation had been stripped away destroying the habitat of many birds and animals.

Before looking at the havoc wreaked that day we will look back across the years to families and fashions of another time.

Residents of Foster Street gather outside Puddy's, their general store on the Robertson Road corner, to celebrate Victory in Europe. Those who can be identified are: Iris Newcombe, far left with dog; Sheila Morgan, next to her; Mrs Puddy stands in front of the shop door giving the Victory sign; Steve Hobday, wearing a tie, is next to the soldier; and slightly in front of him is Mr Francis. Next along is May Hobday in the flowered dress and it is thought the man in the suit is Mr Morgan. In the front row Mr Puddy crouches beside Adolf Hitler! The lady next to him in satin blouse and glasses is thought to be his sister. This picture epitomises the relief felt by countless groups of neighbours all over the country in May 1945.

Clockwise from top left:

A birthday party is being celebrated by Peter Hobday at his home, 1 Foster Street. The children watching him blow out his candles are Peter Coombes on his right, brother Brian on his left and Margaret Morgan. The identity of the other little boy is unknown.

The Godfreys who lived at 13 Foster Street. This is Harry and Lilian with their children Arthur and Lillian May. When Lillian married she only moved down the street as far as No. 1!

A local family pose for a photograph in a Mivart Street garden, *c.* 1920. The couple on the right are Lewis Sutton John and his wife Minnie, with daughter Ethel front right. Their son Herbert stands top right and their other son, Arthur, is in the middle of the front row. Next to Minnie is Mrs Godfrey, whose son Arthur stands behind her. Bottom left is her daughter, Lillian May Godfrey (who later became Mrs Hobday, mother to Peter and Brian in the photograph directly above).

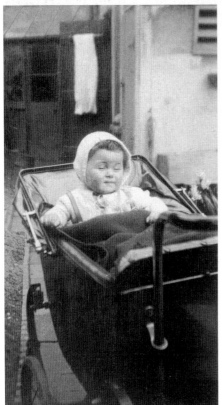

Top: Fire at the factory! This is the day that a blaze began in the Epstein building, an event which caused a surge of spectators in the street. This episode occurred in the late 1930s. It is interesting to note that the top part of Mivart Street was initially known as Mivart Road.

Above and left: Some delightful photographs from the 1920s taken in a garden in Robertson Road. In the picture on the left are some interesting period details like the roller towel on the back of the kitchen door and the vintage pram, which is a joy to behold. These trusty carriages were far more comfortable than today's buggies. In the picture above baby is dressed to kill in a gorgeous bonnet (almost certainly crocheted by hand) and a sweet little matching coat.

Above left: Reaching the toddler stage meant wearing sturdier shoes. These pretty t-straps have a cut-out pattern on the front – just the thing to set off a lace-trimmed frock.

Above right: Bruce Avenue celebrates the end of the Second World War. It is amazing how folk managed to rustle up such delicious cakes at a time when rationing was particularly severe.

Above: A class from Coombe Road School in the 1930s when nearly all little girls seemed to favour bows in their hair. Although the school was demolished a section remains and has been incorporated into a community playgroup in Berkeley Green Road.

Left: The swinging sixties come to Camelford Road as Linda Williams and Jeff Wilkins set off to attend a wedding. In 1966 this was the look to which elegant girls aspired – matching accessories, big hats and long gloves. The couple are still together – married with three sons!

From top:

Greenbank post office, pictured at the time when Maurice Culliford was postmaster there. This picture was taken in February 1982 after a raid had taken place – hence the police presence. Sadly this is no longer serving the local community as a retail outlet. Like so many corner shops it has been converted to domestic use. It used to be a thriving business due to its proximity to the chocolate factory.

The view up Edward Street from the old railway line looking in the direction of Royate Hill. Eastville Girls' School can be seen in the distance.

This less-than-perfect print has been included here because of its rarity value. It seems very few photographs now exist showing the pupils, staff, or even the building of Eastville Girls' School, which is strange when you consider how many girls must have passed through its portals. This picture dates from the mid-1950s. From left to right, back row: Maria ?, Sylvia Starr, Maureen James. Front row: Pat Brian, Joyce Stallard, Barbara Bishop. Perhaps it was their leaving day as there are no red and white-striped uniform dresses in evidence.

The railway arch which crossed Greenbank View. Edward Street is seen through the archway.

Demolition of the bridge in March 1973. The prefabs also went in favour of modern town houses.

Clockwise from top left: Ellen Hoare takes Margaret and baby Janet to visit their auntie in Royate Hill in the 1940s.

The family on the ground behind the houses. This wild land was known as the Spinney – an oasis away from the sounds of the city.

A few years on and Margaret poses in her aunt's garden sporting a shirred elastic bathing costume – the epitome of chic in that era. The beach balls too were an absolute must-have on every little girl's wish-list.

February 1988 and the slopes of Clay Hill live up to their name as building work begins to extend the housing there.

The lovely tree-clad slope prior to the bulldozers moving in.

After the contractors had attempted total clearance of the site in 1992.

The vegetation beginning to grow back in 1993. It is restored now and is a fascinating place for local schoolchildren to study the plants, animals, birds and insects that abound there once more.

This is the Royate Hill action group campaigning by the viaduct. After the hard-fought battle was eventually won and the nature reserve was established there the leaders of the group received a well-deserved award at Buckingham Palace. One of these organisers was the late Mike Purnell, seen on the left of the photograph holding the banner aloft. His wife Claudine is in front holding one of the 'Save Royate Hill now' stickers that were prominently displayed at the time. The *Evening Post* highlighted the endeavour throughout. Age Resource's patron, Sir Fred Holliday, is reported as saying: 'Campaigning is not just fighting and winning battles – it is also losing them and then doing battle all over again. The residents of Royate Hill have done just that with staggering grit and determination. Would that more wildlife in Britain had such plucky protectors!'

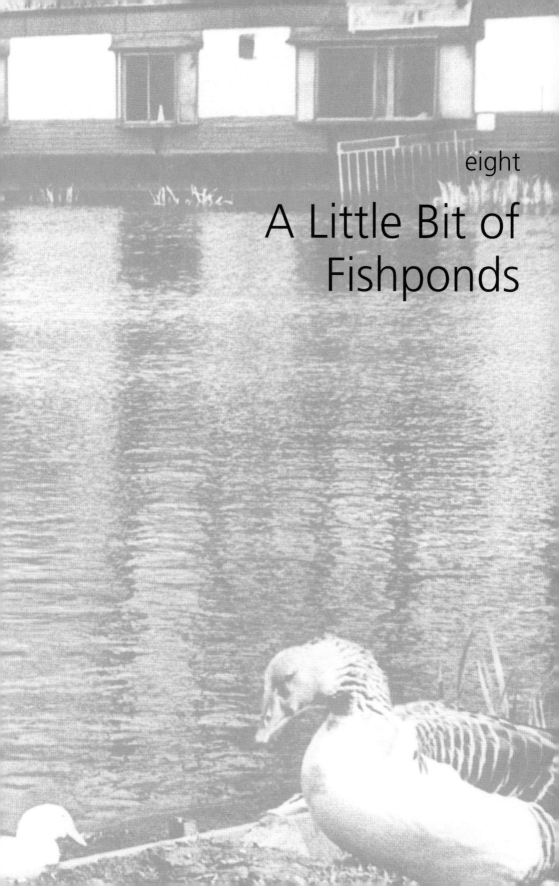

eight

A Little Bit of Fishponds

It is hard to imagine the vast amount of land once owned by the lords of the manor. To consider that the entire Hillfields estate was once a mere 'thicket' belonging to the Duke of Beaufort almost beggars belief. The land was acquired by Bristol Corporation around 1920 at a time when the civic authorities were beginning to take responsibility for rehousing people. Prior to this when dwellings deemed 'uninhabitable' were torn down it was up to the evicted occupants to find somewhere else to live, but when whole blocks were demolished this was often well-nigh impossible. The misery of the people involved can only be guessed at.

Hillfields was, like Sea Mills, a 'model' estate and folk vied for houses there. It was well planned and soon had its own shops, churches, chapels and school. The vast majority viewed it as a home for life and happily lived out their days there.

Building an estate in this position was more realistic than later schemes at, say, Hartcliffe, because the tenants did not feel isolated. There was already an established community in Fishponds itself and, although it might have seemed a bit 'out in the country', it was still only a tram's ride away from the city centre and old haunts. There was also work to be had in the area.

Above left: The wedding of Edward Maggs and Ethel Winter. They made their home in Briar Way, Hillfields. *Above right:* Ethel's brother Harry was a keen gymnast. He was a member of a very successful local team.

On the main Fishponds Road was a branch of the Bristol Co-operative Society whose dividend cards were the forerunner of today's loyalty cards. The building remains but ceased to trade as a branch of the Co-op in the 1970s.

The Imperial Stores, 626 Fishponds Road, disappeared, together with half the rest of the row, to clear a site for the construction of the Benefits Agency building in the early 1970s. Some attractive properties were lost at this time.

Above: The Blackboy, an off-licence at the Fishponds Road end of Forest Road, pictured in the 1950s. In this shot we are granted an intriguing glimpse inside the shop to see the wooden panel which could be unhooked if the window display required dusting and changing. There are some crates stacked near the counter so perhaps a delivery has just taken place. The window still retains some of its old-fashioned china lettering and there is a wide selection of beverages to entice the customers to 'Join Our Xmas Club' as the notice reads. Although today the shop's front still remains, albeit minus the whisky and brandy advertisements, the building is no longer used as a shop.

Left: The prettily-named Strawberry House off-licence in Downend Road, Fishponds. It looks as though it was originally built as a cottage and adapted for retail use. Ales were being sold there as far back as 1899 when the licensee was Matilda Singer, but since then the wheel has turned full circle and it is now a private house once more.

Above: Another licensed premises now converted, in this case to an office, is Seymour House on the corner of Forest Road and Filwood Road. The wall with the post box has gone, as has that on the left with the little wooden gate. Mrs Gladys Hendy ran the business from the 1930s until the 1970s.

Right: Boots the Chemists pictured in February 1957. A ghostly figure stares out at the camera from a window above the shop. In those days the premises were flanked by Dunn and Hopton, gentlemen's outfitters, and Playfair, who supplied the fashion-conscious of the era with Louis-heeled shoes and court peep-toes. Boots now has a rather more eye-catching window display and has expanded by taking over one of the adjoining properties. The other buildings remain but serve different purposes, although there is still a shoe shop next door. This section of Fishponds Road was always known as Cheapside.

The impressive post office, built in the late 1930s to replace the older one that had stood in the block between Station Road and New Station Road. This picture was taken in June 1956. By this time it was no longer used as a post office, and there are signs on the building declaring it about to be developed. The post office now operates from a section in a nearby supermarket.

A scene from the early days of the twentieth century looking up towards the Cross Hands. The wall on the left and the magnificent trees are long gone with the development of the Oldbury Court estate and the shops on Straits Parade. Traffic has also increased somewhat.

Fishponds railway station, an evocative shot reminding us of days when stations had waiting rooms, canopies, attractive gas lamps and a reliable train service. This station, which was extremely well-used, closed down in the 1960s. This local line was a handy means of travelling to Mangotsfield and Warmley.

A redundant police station boarded up in 1976.

The lovely stone building that was Dr Bell's school, pictured in 1962. It was deemed outdated and demolished as so many educational establishments were in the 1960s and 1970s.

Fishponds Lido in September 1968. People flocked here on warm summer days and it was a boon for young mothers with children to keep amused as there was a safe paddling pool there for the younger ones. The place had been converted from an old quarry in what was once Shiner's Fields and some parts of the swimming area were dangerously deep. After a few tragedies here it was decided to close it.

The refreshment rooms on the site in the 1930s. A wonderful array of bentwood chairs can be seen in this photograph.

Right: The restaurant was a favourite venue for wedding receptions. Here the author stands with her cousin Richard and her mother after acting as bridesmaid to her aunt and uncle.

Below: After the closure of the swimming pool there were several attempts to keep things going by establishing a 'floating pub' called The Fisherman which could be hired for functions, but the scheme never really took off and modern housing now covers the land.

Fishponds Park in July 1965 with, perhaps, office workers taking a little fresh air at lunchtime. Readers interested in fashion should note the wide-topped woven bag, a popular accessory of the era.

A look at the Government Training Centre buildings in Vassalls Road on 24 July 1965 brings back recollections of red phone boxes, telegraph poles and vintage cars. It also brings us to the end of our journey back in time around Stapleton. It is to be hoped that some pleasant memories have been stirred in the process.